Remember The Time

A TRUE INTIMATE LOOK AT
MICHAEL JACKSON

Theresa J. Gonsalves

ISBN: 978-0-9762347-4-6
Hardcover - NON-FICTION

Printing services by:
RJ Communications, LLC
51 East 42nd Street, Ste 1202
New York, NY 10017

Copyright© 2009 Theresa J. Gonsalves
Library of Congress Cataloguing in publication data
Gonsalves, Theresa 1958
Remember the Time
Library of Congress Control Number: 2009909843

Cover illustrated by artist David Lloyd Glover
Author Photo by Cedra Stokes

Published by TJG Management Services, Inc., Las Vegas, NV
All publishing rights

Michael Jackson
1958-2009

Acknowledgements

A sincere thank you goes to my number one, Ms. Marlene Frye, for your continuous love and support! I love you my numero uno!

I would also like to thank all my friends & family who have been in my life through thick and thin. Thanks to all who comforted me when I felt like my world ended when Michael's life did:

My son, Mychal Oliver, Lorraine McCollin, (my Rainbow), Kim Coleman, Ayshea Maines, April Washington, Cedra Stokes, my brother Anthony Gonsalves (always Junior to me), the first to break the news to me that Michael Jackson had moved on to eternity, Illiya Clark, Monique Frye, Pamela Lancaster, Adrian Allen, Tesha and Ken Young, Loretta Fonfield, Echo Frye, Vera Barnes, Valerie Bleckler, Irene Coleman, whose friendship was lost along the way but found again and last but not least, Michelle Perlman, who upon just talking to me offered unconditional support. There are so many I can't personally name you all, but please know I do love you!

A very, very special thank you to **Author Moses Miller**, who encouraged me to share my story by making me realize that I was truly one of the lucky ones who was able to share such memories of love with Michael Jackson. Moses Miller is a great author, please support his books!

And thank you Michael & Cathy Angelone of Angelone Builders, for believing in me.

I would like to dedicate this book to everyone who dares to dream big!

Dare to dream it ...
Dare to make it come true!

"Remember the Time"

I decided to write this book to give people a true insight on my personal relationship with Michael Jackson. While our story was told in Star Magazine, Randy Taraborelli's Michael Jackson, the Magic and the Madness and on VH1, they were only told what we wanted them to know and besides, they told it *their* way. It's time I tell it ***my way***.

Michael Jackson and I met because of my letter writing….this book is a series of letters to him in the after life that takes you on a journey through our personal memories that we shared.

So, I invite you to come along with Michael and me to remember the time!

To Katherine Jackson

- I write this with the utmost respect -

On April 28, 1977, I sent these words to Michael Jackson:

"Words are like magic. A writer can show truth in words, when the truth is obscured by happenings. I seek that magic when I write you."

I intend to share that magic with you!

Love, Theresa J. Gonsalves

Sit Back, Relax and Read!

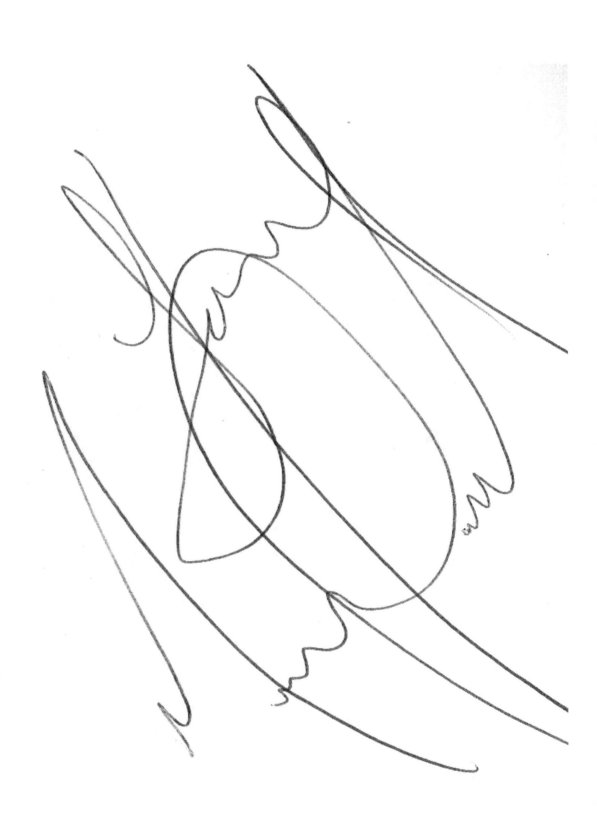

"Letters to Michael Jackson"

Dear Michael,

I sit here wondering what went so blatantly wrong in your life that you had to die so soon. I am wondering why … no screaming loudly inside, "Why? Why? Why?" I feel like some where along the way, I deserted you when you needed me to still be there.

A part of me died with you. Hell, I had you in my life for thirty eight years. I only had my mother for thirty three.

The pain that finally subsided in my chest, immobilized me for days.

I called my stepmother, Midge, a Jehovah's Witness, for help. She comforted me by telling me that perhaps you will have a chance at resurrection and that you are simply resting.

So rest peacefully for now my scarecrow and relax as you read my letters as you once devotedly did and *remember the time we…*

Dear Michael,

I still have the notebooks that I used to keep track of letters I wrote to you so long ago. I wanted each letter to be different so I kept notes about what I wrote you.

As I read through them, I feel the joy, the laughter but mostly the desire I had to just be with you. They journey a lot of the feelings I felt and the things we did. It brings back lots of loving mixed memories.

I moved to Virginia Beach two weeks after you left us. I say us because at that point you belonged to the World.

Janet said, *"To you, Michael was an icon. To us Michael was family."* I felt her pain. Yet, you were my family too. It's always been a constant thought, where would I be if there were no you?

As I stand on the deck of the town home I now live in looking out at the lake, I feel you would have loved it here. It is so peaceful. I came here to write, but my mind is still on losing you. I start thinking back to that first time you and I ever made love. It surprised us both.

The great thing about it was that it wasn't our intention, but sinful nonetheless…

Dear Michael,

From the age of twelve, I just thought you were so cute when my brother, Junior, came home with the Diana Ross presents the Jackson Five album. Funny how I can't recall listening to anyone else's music back then. Well, with the exception of one song by the Temptations – Just my Imagination. I often daydreamed about us to that song (smile).

You were the talk of my seventh grade class. You and Jermaine. So, I decided that I would love Marlon instead. I felt like Marlon wasn't getting any love!

All it took was for one girl to finally say that she loved Marlon, for me to decide it was okay to say it was you that I really liked.

Beginning with that first album, from that beautiful smile, I always knew you and I were destined to meet someday.

I don't remember what I said in my first letters to you. I didn't start keeping my "Letters to Michael" journals until 1974. I do remember in the beginning, I had been mailing letters to you to a post office box, a fan club address.

After writing you many letters to a post office box for almost two years there was a very nice lady in the post office who finally said, "Sweetheart, I am tired of you sending this little boy gifts and letters to a post office box. I am going to tell you how to get his home address!"

What she told me worked. She had explained to me that under the Freedom of Information Act the post office was obligated to give me your home address for one dollar! The first response from the Encino Post office was that they were not a directory. But I wrote back and specifically addressed the information the postal worker gave me and finally this is what they mailed me!

The Jackson 5 reside at

4641 HAYVENHURST AVE
ENCINO, CALIF. 91316

Yes, I saved that too!

Letter to Michael – April 2, 1974

I am enclosing my first 1974 penny to you for good luck. I hope you don't spend it for a while...and who is this guy that is considered the Jackson Five's greatest fan – Donald Ward?

Letter to Michael – June 1974

How come I love you so much and don't really know you? Michael, I hope you don't let some sweet talking girl with a brain turn your head. (I stole that line from a Nancy Wilson song) ...Rumor has it you are coming back to Boston. That's a surprise since you said you were never coming back here. Well you are welcome to stay at our home.

Letter to Michael – July 1974

My mother said you won't write me back because of my last name. I don't know what that has to do with anything. I'm coming to see you in New York.

Dear Michael,

It was July of 1974 when I asked my father to take me to see you in New York at Radio City Music Hall. After being so persistent he finally decided to drive me there. Well, the tears helped too. I had written and told you I was coming and I definitely intended to be there!

We didn't have tickets but before we left, I had called the venue and the venue reps indicated there were plenty of tickets available.

However, of course after the five hour drive from Boston to New York, there were no tickets to be found. My father was ready to just take me back home, but I was adamant that we get tickets from a scalper. I didn't even know what the heck a scalper was at the time. My dad couldn't really afford to pay the money we paid for those tickets! But he knew how much I really wanted to see you.

The seats were horrible! There was no way you could have possibly seen me there! I watched the show, or rather the back of the show. These were nose bleed seats in back of the stage. I cried all the way home. I knew what hotel you were staying in and my dad offered to take me there. I shrugged and told him to just take me home. I felt only groupies went to hotels. I really hoped I didn't disappoint you.

We arrived back at my house at seven o'clock in the morning. I ran upstairs to my bedroom. I laid across my bed still hurt at disappointing you as I wondered if you looked for me. I stared at my blue walls, covered with many pictures of you and your brothers. There were 210 pictures at last count. The sun was shining brightly through the three windows that surrounded my room.

A small record player sat on my dresser. I got up and turned on the Got to Be There album. Once composed, I picked up the phone and called the hotel.

First, I called and asked the hotel operator directly for you. Of course the reply was, "There is no one here by that name." So, I hung up, redialed and asked for Reggie Wiggins. I had read in Right On magazine that Reggie Wiggins was your road manager.

This time …success! Reggie answered the phone. I knew I had awakened him but well…umm…I just didn't care. I wanted to know where you were and if you were upset about my not being where you could see me.

"Mr. Wiggins, I am looking for Michael?"

"He's asleep in the next room."

"Well, I guess you can't wake him up." I stated questioningly.

"No, it's really too early, but I will give him a message, what's your name?"

"Theresa…Theresa Gonsalves from Boston."

"Okay, I will make sure he gets the message," he said and was about to hang up the phone when I noticed on your schedule that you would be in Las Vegas the week of my sixteenth birthday.

"Hey, I have the Jackson Five's schedule in my hand and they're going to be in Las Vegas for my 16th birthday. If I fly to Las Vegas from Boston, do you think I could meet Michael?"

His exact words were, "Honey…if you fly from Boston to Las Vegas, *just* to meet Michael Jackson, I will make sure you meet him. I may not be working with them though but I'll make sure Bill Brey knows, so just ask for Mr. Brey."

"Okay…thank you! Thank you!" my voice now hurrying Mr. Wiggins off the phone as my mind instantly went into planning mode. How was I going to pull this off?

And Michael, as you know, my quest began. I knew we were going to meet in the next few months. It was so on!!!

I will write again tomorrow.

Dear Michael...

Remember I told you I worked after school and saved all my money to buy my own plane ticket. My mom use to make me buy my own school clothes, but this time I opted for no new clothes and instead bought the plane ticket.

It's funny how easy and simple it was back in the day for a fifteen year old to just go to the airport and purchase a plane ticket. No one even questioned me.

I worked hard to save the money for the trip. I had to also maintain good grades to take a week off of school. As I struggled hard to work, do schoolwork and write you letters, I got to a point where I didn't think I would have enough money for the rest of the trip so I started writing letters to every Mayor whose name I could find and asked each of them for a five dollar donation.

Every one of them responded. When I started receiving all this official mail, my brothers thought I had gotten in trouble.

Not one of them sent a dime though! How funny is that! But I worked really hard and came up with the money. Did you know I even wrote letters to the MGM Grand Hotel Presidents' secretary? Her name was Sharon and even she wrote me back. She actually made all my room arrangements and gave me a big suite for next to nothing. I still have a copy of that bill!

Oh, but then came time for me to go. See my mother wasn't taking this seriously. A week before it was time for me to go, she finally asked, "Where exactly do you think you are going?"

"I'm going to meet Michael Jackson," I responded with so much joy and pride.

But then mom dropped a bomb on me, "You are only fifteen years old. What makes you think you can fly across the country to meet Michael Jackson?"

"Well, he knows I am coming," I explained calmly.

"I don't care. You are not going." She looked at me like I was crazy. Uh, I looked back at her like she was the crazy one because, oh, she was so wrong.

I was extremely upset and crying. I had told *everyone* I was flying to Las Vegas to meet you. A few kids in high school had constantly made fun of me about it. In particular, a girl named Karen High. I had good grades and I know I was considered sort of nerdy especially because I wasn't so into the girlie stuff. Some of the kids made fun of me but I was already use to that since seventh grade. That just made me more determined. As they say today, let your haters be your motivators. That was my goal.

And now here was my own mother about to light a match to my dreams.

"Mummy, if you don't let me go, then I will just kill myself."

I said it pretty matter-of-factly. Plain and simple. At that point, I think I meant it. It was an awful and manipulative thing for me to threaten but what else was I to do?

Fortunately for me, Sharon, from the MGM Grand Hotel, called my mother and told her they had arranged for someone to pick me up at the airport and they would make sure I was okay at the hotel.

Whew! Close call. I thought my dream was truly up in smoke. I had worked way too hard to not see it through to fruition.

Talk to you later.

Love you.

Dear Michael,

Do you remember when we first met? Las Vegas, Nevada, November, 1974. MGM Grand Hotel....It's Bally's now. They built a new MGM. Well, you were living in Las Vegas, so you know that.

I had never even been on a plane before! American Airlines, a window seat...I sat balled up in a blanket the entire flight.

A whole week in Las Vegas with your family! Your mom called my mom to tell her she would watch me. Even you, surprised that I had traveled there on my own, asked with astonishment, "Your mother let you come here by yourself?!"

Marlon said, *"If Joe was here, you wouldn't be!"* as he hung up from talking to Carol on the telephone and handed me a bottle of 7-Up. (Would you laugh if I tell you I still have the bottle?!! Well I do...)

I wrote you at least one hundred times from July of that year until we met. I tried to write every day no matter how trivial the events may have been. Actually, I think I only missed one day during that time period.

I sent you copies of my report cards... *"straight A's...I know Michael will be proud of me"* and I wrote of what I felt was sadness in my childhood. I had been working since I was eleven years old. Like you, my childhood had been taken away too. Just yours was done in the public eye, in a much bigger way on a much bigger scale.

Somehow, I sensed you were reading my letters. I can't explain the feelings. Either way, I simply believed it. Then you confirmed it when I called you on the phone in October while you were performing at the Sahara Tahoe Hotel in Lake Tahoe.

Do you think sometimes fate steps in to make things happen?

This time when I had called the hotel, I simply asked to be put through to your room. After asking for you by name, they actually put me through.

Imagine my surprise when you really answered and knew who I was!!! Of course at that point we had never spoken ... other than in my dreams, so, yes, imagine my amazement.
"Hello."

"Hi Michael. This is Theresa"

You hesitated.

"Theresa Gonsalves from Boston…"

"Theresa! Hi!!!" you exclaimed with such surprise, (I am trying to write this how you sounded … lol)

Of course, I was in a state of shock because you actually answered, so I simply said … "Well, I just wanted to let you know that I am coming…"

You cut me off before I could continue.

"I know, I know… you are coming to meet me for your sixteenth birthday. You will be in Las Vegas, November 20th thru the 27th. You have been writing that at the end of all your letters."

I am not sure I can put into words how I felt when you said that. You had just confirmed that you had been reading my letters, at least the ones that I wrote that year. Stunned, I said, "umm, okay bye…"

You laughed then asked, "You don't want to talk?"

"No. No, I will see you when I get there." I responded quietly. I am sure you didn't quite expect that reaction. I hung up the phone, ran to my room, picked up my notebook and went to the Franklin Park Zoo to write you yet and still another letter.

What did I write that made you want to read my letters? You said, "I wanted to meet you because when I read your letters, I feel like you are standing here talking to me."

Later, in New York, Latoya would say, "We learn so much about school and stuff from your letters because we don't get to go."

I am going to go to bed now Michael, I will write again tomorrow… Stay as sweet as you are.

Luv, T-

Dear Michael,

Okay, so where was I …oh yeah, when I arrived in Las Vegas, I left a message for Mr. Brey. (*Hey, it's good to know Mr. Brey is in heaven looking out for you once again*). Mr. Brey told me to meet him in the lobby at six o'clock and to be ready for the first show.

Mr. Brey was a nice man, protective of you, but knew how to handle those who pursued you. He brought me to the table to sit with your mother, DeeDee, Enid and some other people I didn't recognize as being a part of you.

You and I met after the second show in the back elevator. My initial reaction.…I was definitely *not* impressed. In fact, I was very much caught off guard by your attitude.

I don't remember who else was in the elevator besides me, you, Bill Brey, your mom, and a few others, but Bill said,
"Two shows down, twenty-two more to go."
You rather angrily responded with, "Don't knock it Bill. Just don't knock it."

What the heck? You were a kid! Grown ups weren't disrespected like that way back then. Today, however, is a whole different story.

You barked some kind of orders before actually noticing I was in the elevator, a stranger. You bumped your elbow to Bill, in question of who I was. He introduced us.

I was flattered. Your whole demeanor changed and you smiled. We shook hands ever so gently – our first physical contact (smile).
"You actually came. I've been reading your letters."
And with that statement, boy was I overcome with shyness.
"We all have," your mother interjected which caused me to blush as I thought about all the stuff I wrote to her. "I am going to have to call your mother and tell her we will take care of you." And so she did.

It was an amazing week with your family. During the day, sometimes I sat in my room reading while you guys had "school." That would be tutoring with Mrs. Fine, if I recall her name correctly.

Other times, I sat in the room with Reebie, Janet and Stacey. Janet and I played cards a lot. Go Fish!

Reebie had been getting my letters and stories and she had thought I had already met you and had been to the Hayvenhurst house.

"I read the story you sent about winning a contest and you and your friend went to the house to hang out with Michael and Marlon…"

I laughed and explained to her that it was just a story I had made up. I wrote lots of stories for my drama and journalism classes.

I was able to go to every single show once we met. Two shows a night. I saw the show twelve times! Afterwards it was back stage, dinner or something with almost all of your family every night.

Lots of family drama going on back stage. There was the issue about how much money DeeDee was spending…let's see, don't recall who said it, but it was, "We make ten thousand dollars and DeeDee spends ten thousand dollars."

But the biggest event was Jackie's wedding. Yes, A Las Vegas wedding where Jackie married Enid! And I was there.

I remember when I saw Enid the first night at the dinner table in the showroom. I remember feeling like such a plain Jane because Enid was very sexy. I remember she had on this low cut dress with her boobs voluptuously showing. I started feeling maybe that was more your type. Who even knew Jackie had a girlfriend? Jackie was kind of old compared to us though. *(I hope you are sharing good times in heaven with DeeDee and Enid … It is sad they were taken away while so young too. Now, at the very least, you have some of the family women taking care of you.)*

There were these Arabs, sheik or what have you, that had wanted to meet you. You were not interested, so security snuck us out a different way.

When I started to walk out the front door, your mother said, "No, no, no…you look too much like us. You go with us!" I smiled at that. I never thought I looked like a Jackson!

But after your mother had the picture taken with me, you and all of your brothers, I, too, thought, I *do* look just like I fit right in. (smile). I remember telling Ms. Kate that people in the audience were saying that you and Jermaine looked like girls with your hair permed and curled. The next day, my last day, you washed it and had your big afro back!

Latoya had just started performing with the group and she had lots of feelings of inadequacy. She was really nervous. In one show she made a mistake and although I couldn't tell otherwise, she insisted that I could. It didn't matter how many times I saw that show, I would not have caught the error. She said, "I know you saw me mess up, you were looking right at me." For real though Michael, I didn't notice at all.

I think we should get some sleep now. Keep smiling as you read. Everyone misses you.

Dear Michael,

Remember, our last night? November 27, 1974, we sat in that dressing room, just the two of us in Las Vegas. I had turned sixteen during that week.

Jackie, Jermaine and Marlon tried to make us kiss! They held both our hands behind our backs and told us to kiss. You shyly danced your way loose.

Everyone went to dinner. Why do I remember this like it was yesterday?!

I had heard you tell your mother that you didn't want to go eat, so I decided I was going to just stay wherever you were.

So here we were.

First you sat there reading your Bible. I sat there fidgeting, knowingly doing whatever I could do to distract you.

You finally started laughing. So, you were intentionally ignoring me huh!

And then who would have thought these next words would come out of your mouth, "Do you believe in the devil?"

I must admit Michael, *that* actually scared me because I didn't have a clue where you were going with that? But of course you followed with all you were learning and began sharing your knowledge of God with me.

I felt kind of stupid about it all, because although I had grown up going to Catholic Church, I wasn't aware of any of what you were telling me. You read me the scripture, *"Matthew 24:7-For nation will rise against nation and kingdom against kingdom and there will be food shortages, pestilences and earthquakes in one place after another"* ... as you spoke relevant to the time of the end of this system.

I pray that you get that chance at resurrection Michael.

I am trying so hard not to be sad at losing you.

Dear Michael,

I was getting pretty teary eyed when I was writing about our last day together in Las Vegas. Each passing day, I am coming to grips that your shell, your body, won't dance about on this earth any more, but your soul is still surrounding my heart.

Anyway, our conversation about God lasted for about an hour.

Then suddenly, out of the blue you jumped out of the chair, with alarm and said, "I just can't believe your mother let you come here by yourself. Let's call her."

I started laughing as we dialed the number to call her. But she wouldn't talk to you. I kept saying, "Mom, just say hi to him…" "Hi, Theresa's mom" you yelled into the receiver.

"I already spoke to his mother; I don't need to talk to him." I think she was just nervous.

Our conversation afterwards just bordered on silly things sixteen year olds talked about…back then that is…today's sixteen years olds sure talk about a lot more than we did. You told me, "I like that you put numbers on the envelopes when you write. When I get home, I know which one to read first."

You also asked me another peculiar, unanticipated question that evening as well, *"Do you want to be a millionaire?"* To which I didn't respond. I had never thought much about it.

I was amazed that you asked me about things I wrote you, such as what was going on in my school, my work and even my high school basketball team! We were in that small dressing room for two hours! Then everyone came back. It was show time.

"This is your last day huh?" you asked.

"Yeah. I'm going home in the morning."

"Too bad we didn't do this sooner. I was just getting to know you better."

We hugged, we smiled, still so very shy, the both of us.

When you got on stage, your shyness went away. You made me feel incredibly special by singing songs to me, making faces like you were sad I was leaving and teasingly waving when you were singing Never Can Say Goodbye!

And then that brother of yours, *Marlon,* pulled me on the stage to dance with you guys on Dancing Machine!!

At the end of the evening, your mom, Reebie, DeeDee and Latoya walked me to the elevator and asked if I would meet them in the morning.

They had wanted to take me shopping for my birthday. I told them I was leaving, but what a nice gesture that was on their part. Or was I just that homely. LOL. They had thought I had one more day to spend with the family but sadly it was time for me to head home.

When I arrived back in Boston, would you believe the very next day, and I mean the *very* next day, the Jehovah Witness' knocked on my door and I started studying with a wonderful lady named Aida Booth.

She would be the one to later tell me, "Do not mistake lust for love!"

I have never forgotten her advice.

Dear Michael,

Of course I didn't stop writing you after we first met. In fact, my letters probably increased. I started writing Latoya a lot as well. Sometimes you wrote back, Latoya wrote back and DeeDee wrote back. My letters from you were stolen, but I still have a couple of letters from Latoya and DeeDee. Here is one from Latoya that I find quite interesting.

Hello Theresa,

I'm sorry it took me a while to write back, but I never got around to it.

Theresa I'm really surprised to know that you you believe Michael has been saying all those things that girl has been making up. You meet Michael. You spent a week with us. You should know what type of person he is. Michael has only two things on his mind. That's Religion and his Music. He doesn't have time for anything else besides his buds and he will tell anybody that.

Be always hear stories like that.

I don't know why people deliberately make up false accusation about someone and no that there not true. Its really a shame people make up such derogatory stories and have people believing in them. I guess its just some thing you have to over look in people.

Theresa I'm sorry to hear that you us not studying any more. Maybe you will start again some day. At least I hope so. I know its hard for you to believe that there is going to be a world free from crime, famine, etc. But God can't let this system continue the way it its. Because man

will only make things
worst the way it has been
for years. He has given man
all this time to inplore the
condition of the world and
theyonly seem to make
things worst. It onlyproves
that man can't do it alone
he need Gods help.
Say he to your friend
Lorraine

Well Theresa I'm going
to say goodbye for now.
Hope to hear from you soon
And try not to believe every
thing you hear. Try
to find them out for
yourself or from
me.

Love
Sister
Jackson

In case you can't read your sister's handwriting, I interpreted it for you:

Dear Theresa,

I'm sorry it took me a while to write back, but I never got around to it.

Theresa I'm really surprised to know that you believe Michael has been saying those things that girl has been making up. You meet Michael. You spent a week with us. You should know what type of person he is. Michael has only two things on his mind. That's his Religion and his Music. He doesn't have time for anything else besides his birds and he will tell anybody that. We always hear stories like that. I don't know why people deliberately make up false accusations about someone and no that there not true. It's really a shame people make up such derogatory stories and have people believing in them. I guess it's just something you have to overlook in people.

Theresa I'm sorry to hear that your not studying anymore. Maybe you will start again someday. At least I hope so. I know it's hard to believe that there is going to be a world free from crime, famine, etc. But God can't let this System continue the way it is because man will only make things worst the way it has been for years. He has given man all this time to improve the conditions of the world and they only seem to make things worst. It only proves that man can't do it alone. He needs God's help.

Say hi to your friend Lorraine.

Well Theresa, I'm going to say goodbye for now. Hope to hear from you soon and try not to believe everything you hear. Try to find them out for yourself or from me.

Love Latoya Jackson

When I read Latoya's letter back from 1975, I realize that your public persecution began a lot earlier than I could possibly have imagined. There were untrue things being said about you even back then and for a moment, I was buying into them. I never did again. I guess I just couldn't see it or even understand it at that young age.

After I read this letter, I had to try to figure out what Latoya was referring to and I realized from the notes in my journal that there was this girl that had been calling me and saying a lot of things about you that just didn't sound right but she had all my information.

We later found out there was a girl named Celeste who had been going through your mailbox, stealing your mail. So I thank Latoya for clearing that up for me and teaching me a lesson.

From that point on, I only believed words I heard of whom I knew you to be.

Dear Michael,

I had your schedule for 1975. Once again you were going to be performing in New York City in July. This time, I made sure we had tickets before we headed there. My oldest brother, Tony (Junior) and his then girlfriend, Darlene, drove me and my best friend, Lorraine, to New York.

After we arrived and we found our seats, I told my brother, "I'm going back stage to say hi to Michael. Do you want to go?" His reply was, *"Yeah right."* He was definitely not a believer.

Well Michael, you know, whenever I said it, I meant it. I went to the first security guard I saw and asked, "Can you please go get Bill Brey?" As fate would have it once again, out of all the security guards that were at the venue, this guy knew who Bill Brey was and easily obliged. Can you imagine that? There were hundreds of security guards on duty and I picked one who knew Bill Brey!

When Bill Brey saw me, it was with instant recognition. Don't believe I really expected that. It had been almost eight months since Las Vegas.

"Hey, Theresa, how are you?" Bill Brey exclaimed, "Michael will want to see you. Come on." I didn't even have to ask!

When we walked in, you were fully dressed in costume, big afro colorful outfits. I spotted you immediately and ran right into your arms for a great big hug almost catching you off guard. I introduced you to Lorraine who was speechless and couldn't even get out a response!

Then Marlon said, "Hey, ain't that the girl from Boston who spent a week with us in Las Vegas? How can she afford to come to these places?" Why was he asking that?

Backstage that evening was a lot of hustle and bustle and you guys were already late going on stage. So we said goodbye, knowing we would see each other again some how and went back to our seats to watch the show. We had missed the first group already, but of course seeing you was well worth the loss.

"Where were you?" my brother asked.

"Backstage, saying hi to Michael" I responded.

"Yeah right…" Neither he nor his girlfriend believed us!

Well come to think of it, I forgot to tell you, when I got back home from Las Vegas, no one at school believed me either! They said I stayed out of school for a week and had the pictures made. Could we even do that back then?

Dear Michael,

Again, I ask, do you believe in fate? It had been quite some time since I had seen you, yet I was still writing to you.

Many things had happened. In 1976, I had my first boyfriend that I cried to you about in my letters. You know the story, Kevin…my first love, second to you. I also graduated from Boston Technical High School with honors and an outstanding achievement award in English. Mostly because of all the stories I had written about us!

By 1977, I was working a full time job and going to business school. It had been two years. I decided it was time to see you again. I knew you were living in New York filming the Wiz. Plus, I knew it was just you and Latoya.

I was still sending letters to Encino and I didn't have an address to where you were staying in New York. I decided I was going to take the train to New York and find you.

I guess I had already proven to be bold by flying to Las Vegas at the age of fifteen. Here I was now, what, eighteen or nineteen, and decided to get on the Amtrak and head straight to New York!

Well, here is where fate steps in for a second, no third time. I arrived in New York City really late at night and I didn't have the faintest idea of where to begin looking for you.

I figured you had to be near Park Avenue somewhere because that is where I had read rich people lived. I flagged a cab. When the cab driver asked where I wanted to go, I simply said, "Can you take me to where Michael Jackson is staying?" Surprisingly he said, "Oh yes, I heard he was staying on Sutton Place." Now how incredible was that?! Of all the cab drivers in New York, I was able to get one who knew exactly where you lived! I would call that a little more than fate. It was the universe saying I belonged with you.

Sutton Place, 400 East 56th Street, Apt 37L, high rise building, doorman and all. I had gotten a hotel room about a block down and waited until the next morning to seek you out. I simply left the picture of us in Las Vegas with the doorman. Then you called and invited me over! That was great!

I am going to close here for now. I keep smiling as I sit back and remember the time we….

Dear Michael,

We were so young...lol, and if I say, *"and innocent"* I will start singing the song. (smile).

It was a surprise to your sister, Latoya, each time you had invited me to your penthouse apartment in New York. At first, I didn't understand her hesitancy when she had been writing me back often after we had met in Las Vegas. I brought my friend Lorraine with me one time.

I thought it was so cute that you had made me some cookies and opened the door smiling holding the plate of cookies in your hand.
"I made you some cookies! Chocolate chip" you smiled. You were so proud that you had made them yourself. We were almost twenty years old. Had you not baked cookies before?

When I looked at you, we started laughing because it brought memories of when you were a kid and you use to say "I gave you my cookies" before singing Who's Loving You! That started an evening of hilarity.

Almost everything from that point on was just so funny to us, except when we had that conversation about child abuse. Yeah, you made me cookies and I brought you a book. "Somewhere a Child is Crying."

People don't really understand that even when you were young, you had that desire to save the children of the world. We talked for hours about child abuse and exchanged horror stories about what we read and heard, from children being burned by their parents, to other outrageous abuses.

While we chatted about this, the doorman buzzed in and said that there were two fans there to see you who had been coming over every single day. Your frustration with them was apparent as you told me, "These girls follow me wherever I go. I asked if I could bring you to the set of the Wiz and they told me no, but I turn around and I see *them* there. Diana Ross yelled at them. She told them...Leave him alone! Can't you see he is busy?" You laughed mimicking Diana's voice, but your annoyance was apparent.

So, I made a suggestion…. "Just let them come up Michael. Maybe after they meet you it won't be so bad…." You weren't a believer of that but you decided to humor me anyway.

Do you remember what happened then? Our silliness took over when they got in the room. We went back to our conversation about child abuse and when one of the girls started telling this unbelievable story that she seemed to have made up, you sat there making faces at me. They couldn't see you. We busted up laughing out loud in the midst of her story and she angrily stated, "I don't know why you two think this is so funny…" We were bad Michael, and rude, but we just couldn't help it that day! Hmm, perhaps it was our nerves?

You suggested we take pictures. Again you continued with the silliness and only you and I were getting in the pictures when one of the girls asked, "Where do you two think you're at? Picture land or something?" …that just added to our hysteria. We looked at each other and busted up laughing again! We were out of control.

When I get really sad that you are gone, I go to YouTube and look at the video of your doing an interview in Japan where you can't stop laughing. It floods me with memories of this day and takes away some of the pain of your death. Laughter, it truly does help to heal.

Wow…you're really gone.

Dear Michael,

After my first visit to New York, we spent hours on the phone late at night for a couple of weeks and then you invited me back. It was November or December. I know it was cold. The first day I was there, I barely got to see you because you were working so much on the set of the Wiz.

The second morning after you left for work, Latoya quietly gave in and let me stay at the apartment with her. She was mad that you weren't listening to anything she was instructing. You were really antagonizing her as any normal brother would. You know it scared the hell out of her when you played around hanging off that damn balcony. I would have been scared too. I'm really glad you didn't do that in front of me.

As I spent the day with Latoya, I was able to figure out why she was so disappointed that you invited me to visit. She was trying to help Stephanie Mills get you. I don't think Latoya knew that I was listening in on her tête-à-tête with Stephanie when she told Stephanie to buy you a book.

Apparently, Stephanie had wanted to buy you a gift and asked Latoya what she should get you. I chuckled to myself because I had already done that. I already knew what you liked. I didn't have to get that information from your sister!

I also heard Latoya telling Jermaine that she didn't want to go out with Bobby DeBarge. She did tell me after she got off the phone that Jermaine wanted her to date Bobby and that she was only telling me because I was sitting there and heard the conversation. I was so very nosey.

She said Jermaine had founded the group Switch, that Bobby was a part of, and he wanted her to be nice to him. Hmm, I could have interpreted that so many different ways. But I always looked at things so innocently then. She asked me not to tell anyone. I obliged…well until now that is, here I am telling you. So don't tell her I told you okay (smile)?

Dear Michael,

Do you remember how tired you were when you came home that evening from the set of the Wiz? I was anxious just for you to get back. We talked a lot about your day because you were so excited about the day's event, that it was hard for me not to get caught up in your excitement.

We didn't even eat. We just talked. We joked about my favorite song at the time which was Find Me a Girl. We laughed as you told me how you didn't even know what you were going to say when your brothers chimed *"What you gonna do?"* and ended up with *"I'm gonna be good to her."* We were laughing at the way you said 'I'm gonna be'. I still chuckle when I hear that.

You decided I would sleep in your bed that night and you would sleep on the couch although I had a small hotel room down the street. You hadn't wanted me to be there alone when I had come to see you and you had been gone all day. We talked some more until we decided we better go to bed. You needed to be rested for the next day's shoot.

However, we both couldn't sleep. I could hear you moving about and then you got up to use the bathroom. The bathroom was just off your bedroom.

Your room was really small, not what most people would have imagined you having. You only had a twin size bed while Latoya's room was very luxurious. She had a big bed with a mirror above it.

I laid in your bed listening to you pee. When you came out the bathroom, I saw you glance in at me and you saw that I was awake too, "You can't sleep either huh?" I asked you as I put my head up.

You smiled at me and came in the room, closing the door behind you. You sat in the chair at your desk which was next to your bed. You again expressed how really excited you were about the set that they had built for you as the scarecrow on the set of the Wiz. I sat up because you wanted to proudly show it to me again. You had shown me earlier.

I got out the bed and stood next to you putting my arm around your waist as you pointed out features of the replicated set. I was simply taking in your joy. When I let you go, I leaned in to look closer at what you were showing me, we ended up face to face. The pull of the chemistry ... it was like it was just supposed to happen, that we kissed. Had we not found ourselves in this position earlier and Latoya had walked in? This time there was no distraction. It was a soft surprise kiss to us both as we explored each others mouths gently with our tongues.

We both felt shy, but it didn't stop what we knew was going to happen and what we both wanted to happen. You took my hand and we got in your bed together both with our heads down. We were mutually quite shy.

I wondered how many other girls you had been with, if any. What about your religion? Weren't you the one who sent *me* to seek God?

Other than what you read in my letters, sex was never even something we had discussed. If you were still reading my letters, you knew I had been with one other guy. Even then, I felt as if I had betrayed you. But my letters never stopped and you knew my heart was still where you were. Were you shaking more than I was?

We laid there silently embracing, neither of us being the aggressor, as I just let you hold me in your arms. I can still remember feeling the warmth of being there. It was so quiet in your room that all we could hear was our hearts beating. We knew Latoya was in her room not too far away so we were being careful not to make a lot of noise. As far as I knew, the door to the bedroom was unlocked.

You were so nervous. Well I was too, but you seemed more so than I. Funny thing is we were both sure we wanted it to happen, but so unsure of ourselves. Our kissing was slow. We were learning. You said I had soft lips. I was rubbing your arm thinking, for as skinny as you were, you sure had some muscles.

Our body language was awkward as we responded to one another and we became aroused. You unbuttoned my pajamas and yes it was a flannel pajama set I had on that I was embarrassed about when I went to pull down the pants. Your hands on my breast were hot, but soft. I was afraid to touch your penis. But you took my hand, directing me there as I wrapped my fingers around it and gently rubbed.

When it seemed we were ready, I guided you inside of me as I stared right into your eyes. I remember I wasn't so nervous anymore. We didn't use any protection. We didn't exactly plan this. It was gentle, it was loving, but most of all it was with you ... the young man of all my life, my letters, my dreams.

I didn't get to sleep in your arms all night. I regret that. We whispered quietly afterwards. You asked if I was okay with what happened and I asked if you were. We both smiled as we responded positively to each other. A night we will never forget. I couldn't have loved you any more than I already loved you at that moment.

Letter to Michael - January 26, 1978

Dear Michael,

I thought of you throughout the day today. My love for you is like Gloria's love for Richie Rich. I read an article today in the Boston Globe about you and Stephanie Mills. Says she left you after going steady with you for a year and a half. We know better than that!

That note reminds me of all the comic books I use to send you! I must have sent you hundreds of books!

Letter to Michael – February 12, 1978

Dear Michael,

I am sitting in the window looking out at the stars and thinking of you. The stars are mysterious and their twinkle is like a wink. Our town is still under a state of emergency so I get another day off work. I have cleaned everything, talked on the phone, worked out my budget and my budget allows me to see you sooner than I thought. We need to start over. I have been exercising and working on becoming glamorous for you. My body has more stretch and flexibility which I am sure you'll admire since soon my body will be able to match your every movement. I love you Michael.

Dear Michael,

You called me often on the telephone a lot after I went back to Boston and we would talk about parties you were invited to and attended. You particularly told me about Studio 54 and the fun you had there. So many new things you were exploring there.

I don't quite remember when you went back to California, but you asked me to visit.

And of course, all you had to do was ask! Well hell, I came even if you didn't ask. (LOL). I loved you so very much.

Two weeks before you breathed your last breath, I made this statement to my niece Monique... "I want to live long enough to see Michael Jackson die". When I said it, I imagined you would live a long, long time. To say forever would be foolish.

I couldn't imagine life without you on this earth whether I ever physically saw you again or not. Who could truly imagine you gone? I am still in disbelief.

I was hoping to live long enough to see you die, because your dying was an unimaginable thing. Because of my liver problems, if I outlived you, that meant I would live long too.

What kind of shit was that for me to say? Now it's almost as if it I gave myself permission to die. But no, I am still fighting my illness, Michael. Telling the angels no, heaven can wait.

Dear Michael,

Even after we spent time together in New York, people didn't believe the time I spent with you. None of that mattered as I headed for another visit to California. I was able to spend an entire week there in California with you.

It was then that you had recently gotten your drivers license and we went riding around Encino in your Rolls Royce. You drove out the gate, stopping to say hi to the fans that had been sitting outside. Then you made a slow left turn onto Hayvenhurst. As you proceeded to make that right turn onto Ventura Blvd, by Gelson's, you hit the daggone curb! That was just your first moving violation of the evening. I knew I was in trouble! Okay, I admit it, I was really nervous because right after that you almost hit a car in front of us and you started laughing. Oh yes, I was talking to God for sure at that time.

We had a great time that week. You drove me through Encino and Tarzana, going through the Clark Gable Estates…being silly, stopping the car and playfully telling me to get out and steal some kids' toy that was in front of their home.

Then you drove me over to Quincy Jones house. His house was dark. It was really late but you didn't care. We rang the bell. No one answered.

We had the laughs again and it reminded us of New York and oh, oh … how bad were we sitting there making fun of the Al Green grits incident and cracking up! We talked about how impressed we were with the movie Sybil starring Sally Field. We both loved that psycho stuff!

We had dinner at what was then called Dupar's, where the waitress asked if you were Michael Jackson! Even after you said yes, she asked again as she served you that chicken pot pie you picked over. It wasn't so hard for you back then. I guess you weren't that thriller to everyone else just yet huh! To me, you already were so much more!

After dinner we went to see a Burt Reynolds movie called Hooper. Why did we get shy when some nudity was displayed on the screen? We looked at each other nervously and we both drifted back to that evening we spent in bed together. We smiled apprehensively at each other. I wonder why we had gotten so shy about it. We hugged and kissed in the movie theater. I don't even really remember what the movie was about.

Your mom was the best! First she drove me down Hollywood and Sunset Boulevards to go sight seeing. She showed me where some famous people lived such as your favorite, Diana Ross. Afterwards she took me to the set of Good Times to see Janet taping. Janet was taping an emotionally charged molestation scene.

Janet was so cool and so very talkative. When we were back stage, I remember asking her how she made herself cry on cue and she replied, "I think about Michael dying. It only works with Michael and my mother though." To say I was surprised to hear that would be an understatement. I guess you have to put yourself in that mode somehow.

I really appreciated your mom taking time out of her schedule to take me sightseeing, out to dinner and to see Janet. Strange though for all the time I was able to spend with you, I had yet to meet your father.

We snuck in stolen kisses throughout this visit. At the end of my visit you told me, "You need to move here. I think you should move here!"

Were you reaching out then? Looking for real friends? Anyway, again, all you had to do was ask and I was on my way. See you soon Michael.

Letter to Michael – Sept 22, 1979

Dear Michael,

I am frightened about leaving Boston. They say at eighteen I was considered a woman but I am about to be twenty-one and I feel I am just a baby. If I am so grown up, how come I am still holding on to this dream of our being together and if letting go of you does have something to do with growing up then I don't want to. What's with your new look? Just be yourself. I will call you later.

Dear Michael,

Why was it after I moved to California, things changed? They didn't change in the beginning. I had fears about being there. I only had an uncle there and you. When I started feeling like I wanted to go back home, I showed up at your home, uninvited.

As I walked up to the gate, you were pulling out, but you stopped the car when you saw me and told me to get in.

"I'm on my way out. Are you okay?" You were so concerned.

"Well, I'm thinking about moving back to Boston." I was ready to cry, feeling like a quitter.

"No!" you told me emphatically, "Don't leave until you talk to me. Can you come over on Thursday? Be here at seven."

"Alright, I will" I responded as you reached over and hugged me. Your hugs always made me feel safe.

After I got out the car, the fans that had been sitting at your gate, a regular scenario, quickly encircled me asking, "Why did Michael Jackson ask *you* to get in his car? ...Who are you?"

Tough crowd, your fans.

... "Just a friend of his. Just a friend" was all I could say and leave as quickly as I could.

What happened the next day was a little rough, so I am going to stop for now and pick up tomorrow.

Rest well, my Michael.

Dear Michael,

Well, what happened that Thursday was a series of events that were without reason. Well, your dad was the problem. It's funny or perhaps I should say sad, how you look back on it and realize this was a crossing point for us.

When I arrived at the gate Thursday evening, after a long bus ride from Long Beach to Encino, I was quite annoyed when no one answered and there weren't any lights illuminating from the house.

I foolishly waited for over an hour, but mostly because the buses had stopped running and I didn't know how I was going to get back to Long Beach.

I was at the end of my patience when suddenly a limo pulled up and out jumped Randy. He grabbed my hand and said, "Come on get in. Michael said if you were still here to give you some money and for you to go stay down the street at the Travel Lodge and come over in the morning. He's sorry. Joseph made him go to this event that he didn't want to go to." He stuck some cash in my hand.

It was all so hurried, as they, Randy and Janet, jumped out of the car and ran up the driveway to the house. I got in the car and was taken to the Travel Lodge.

As I slept at the lodge that night, I wondered curiously, why you even wanted me to stay in California.

Who would have thought that all this was going on while you were working on some of your best selling work!

Whew…well when I got there the next morning, hmm, sometime around eleven, Joseph was in the driveway washing his car! Not sure if he saw me, but I rang the bell anyway. No answer, so I rang it again of course as I was becoming agitated. *You* were the one who told me you wanted to talk to me instead of leaving! *You* told me to come by in the morning!

Your mom came down the driveway in her brown Mercedes Benz (Did they use the real one in the American Dream movie, because it looked identical?) and she said, "Michael wanted me to tell you he is sorry. He will try to be out in a little bit."

The journals I kept of "Letters to Michael" –
Can't believe I still have these!

The Jacksons plus me! At sixteen, I made this dream come true!
The hair..the outfits - Wow
That's me in the middle looking like I fit right in.

Remember our last night in Las Vegas! It was fantastic!
This was the dressing room we sat in alone for two hours!

You said this was your favorite picture of us! New York...when we had the giggles...just as Toya was about to snap, someone asked if we thought we were in pictureland or something! LOL

Your bright idea…"Let's pretend we just met!"
Hey look you are holding one of those cookies you made for me!

Okay, in this picture you decided we would try to act serious
instead of laughing as much as we did that evening! I don't
think we did a great job of acting this time! Smile.

Sibling love….You don't look like you were driving her crazy hanging over the balcony and doing whatever you wanted to do! Look at Latoya's nails!

Latoya, I was a better match for Michael than Stephanie!

I love this picture of you and my best friend Lorraine! She is still a rainbow in my world!

The Jackson Five Softball
Team 2005

"Okay, but I feel like Michael needs to apologize to me himself." I was adamant that you were going to do that.

"I agree" she said and drove off.

After a few minutes, I rang the bell again.

Joseph finally opened the gate and asked me to come into the long driveway that leads to the house. This, only after someone in the house, perhaps you, said something to him about me.

He didn't let me in any further than his car. Instead he told me you couldn't see me. Well, for some reason, he didn't really frighten me. He wasn't my damn father. Oh he looked intimidating enough and funny thing after all this time I had spent with you in the past, I had never even met him before. You and I were adults. Or so I thought.

And after all Michael, we made love together, so what anyone else said didn't really matter to me unless it was coming from you.

When he told me you couldn't see me, I possessively replied, "Well, you tell Michael to tell me he won't see me. He's a grown man. Why don't you just leave him alone and let Michael be Michael."

Uhhh … yuh, that sure as hell set him off! Remember… and I say remember because you and Latoya were watching the whole thing through the security cameras…he grabbed me by my arm and yelled, "Just because you spent some time with him in New York and just because he took you out to dinner and the movies a few times doesn't mean you are his girlfriend!" My arm was hurting as his fingers dug in.

"I didn't say I was!" I yelled back at him, trying to free myself from his grip.

And then your mean ass father grabbed me and pushed me out the gate. Yes, I knew it was definitely time for me to go.

I didn't cry, but I wanted to. I was defending you. I was really mad at you too at this point. Why didn't you come to *my* defense? I thought you had gotten out of his clutches. I imagine you really were still afraid of Joseph. You were starting to loosen his grip but hadn't quite made it out as of yet.

I walked slowly towards Ventura and when I got to the corner of at Hayvenhurst, I turned around and saw you and Latoya pass by me in her yellow convertible Mercedes Benz. She had the top down. While I saw you, you didn't see me. I knew you were looking for me.

Dear Michael,

"I snuck out the house with Latoya to come and look for you" you told me as we stood in the middle of Boys Market a few days later. Was Joseph gone by then? It had taken you a few days to call. I was still angry. Did you not ask me to move to California?

"Yeah, well why didn't you just come out?" I asked.

"Because Joseph was there!" you emphasized.

As you said that, I was taken back to when we first met in Las Vegas, when Marlon had point blank stated, "If Joe was here, you wouldn't be."

"We are twenty one years old, why would you need permission?"

"I know, I know...I'm really sorry!" you exclaimed.

"Well, yeah right Michael" I said with total disregard and walked away.

But of course not without being harassed by some of your fans who overheard our conversation.

"Do you know who that is?" one fan asked but didn't wait for a response... "That's Michael Jackson, how dare you talk to him like that!"

"I don't give a damn who he is! He's just a normal person to me." I did feel defeated.

Besides, Michael, we had made love. Did that not matter to you anymore? I learned later that it did, because, New York, wasn't to have been our only time! But, I was quite saddened after that incident.

Dear Michael,

After that occurrence, I didn't quite know how to look at us any more. I rented a house about three miles away from you on Nestle Ave, just off Ventura, east of Reseda Blvd. I decided it was time to let go of you a little. I went back to study with the Jehovah Witnesses.

Actually, I became roommates with two baptized sisters who had moved to California from another state. I went to some of the meetings. Not all. I enjoyed going. Then crazy things started to happen that disillusioned me.

I don't remember ever seeing you or your family at the Kingdom Hall. I felt it disrespectful to look for you there where you were seeking God. I did see the family, Reebie in particular, at the Assemblies sometimes that were held at that big Assembly Hall in Woodland Hills.

Funny, how I was so respectful about some things, but ignorant about others.

I became disenchanted with the Jehovah's Witnesses when my roommates started doing so many inappropriate things…one started dating a married man, one was just crazy and threatening to kill us all the time. She needed some serious medication. My study teacher, Candy, stopped showing up after borrowing money from me and never paying it back.

And then there was the only eligible bachelor in the Kingdom Hall, Vern who was accused of embezzling money from Bank of America. LOL…I know every church has its problems, but this was really getting to me. So one day I decided to never go back. I decided I was going to just enjoy life and do whatever the heck I wanted to do.

I was still writing you letters though. You were still reading them.

Dear Michael,

We didn't lose each other just yet though. Do you remember that little quaint book store in Encino, not too far from your house up by Newcastle Avenue? I think you went there to find solace. You would stay in there for hours. How you just loved to read! When I look through my notebooks, I realize, I must have sent you an entire library of books!

We ran into each other often at that bookstore or we would just plan to meet there or Genesta Park. We would sit in the park a lot and just talk. We called Genesta Park the little park. It is just across from the Encino Post office. We called it the little park relative to Balboa Park being the big park. That was a time when you could go out on your own to a certain degree. People recognized you often, but didn't flock to you like bees to honey.

I'm reminiscing and looking at pictures of you on line and in magazines that I saved. I see that you got that beautiful cashmere scarf that I sent to the Rainbow Theatre in London in Feb of 1979. I didn't want you to be cold. You had it on in a picture.

Are you cold in that casket sweetheart? Wish I could keep you warm. I am going to stop here…my heart is crying for you again.

Dear Michael,

It's been over two months since you left us...People are still speculating all over the place. Of course, some are speechless over losing you...but that damn media ... just won't quit dogging you around. \

I am saddened about the drugs Michael. You were so against drugs, so against them. Sadly, I understand. I totally understand. I don't condone it, but I understand the feeling of the Propofol.

My liver disease keeps me medicated with pain meds and having numerous surgical procedures. I am about to have another one. I had the pain meds too...Lortab, Vicodin, Oxycodone, etc. Yup, I had them all.

I remember my doctor once saying, "I don't want you to get addicted to these pain meds." I looked at him and said, "You don't have to worry about my getting addicted to those. It's the going under that I am getting hooked on. I am loving that affect!" My doctor just thought I was crazy Michael, yet I was so very serious when I said it.

I think about your kids a lot. I remember the time I met them in Las Vegas. It was also the first and only time you met my son Mychal whom I named after you. He was 14 years old then...he is about to be 19 now. I know in time your children will be okay with your family.

Now that you are with God, I am missing you because now I know I can truly never see you again until I reach glory with you.

Just recently I had been telling my friends, "It's time for me to see Michael again..." I told them I was going to wait until after the "THIS IS IT" tour to get in touch with you.

I waited too long.

Dear Michael,

Do you remember, 1983, Balboa Park over by the baseball diamonds when you laid on the grass and picked up my oldest son Todd and held him playfully in the air with your feet? Yeah, my kid, the kid behind the song you told me you wrote about me. He wasn't quite two yet. I wished he was ours. Can you believe he is twenty-seven years old now?

While I thought it was sweet that you wrote a song for me, it wasn't a situation I wanted the world to know about that was for sure! What woman wants the world to know that some man is saying their kid isn't his....Well other than the women on the Maury Povich show!...Did that make you laugh? I use to be able to make you laugh. We laughed so much when we were together.

Billie Jean!!! Together we were amused by all the speculation. But so many things had changed between us at the time. Did we grow apart or did I just grow up? Good question huh?

When I stopped writing you as much as I use to, at the time, I called myself letting go of the fantasy of you. Besides, I lived close by; I had access, so why bother writing so much any more. What I didn't realize at the time was that it was the writing that connected the dots between us.

I called myself trying to become a bad girl after I stopped studying the Bible. After I had told you my plight of being pregnant, the next time I saw you, you said matter-of-factly, "I wrote a song for you, about you." I was flattered before I heard the song. But when I heard the song, I was like, "No he didn't!" So yes, let the people speculate.

I want to clarify to you that you *never* became one of many. But Michael....*Billie Jean*...when you told me about the song, who the hell would have thought it would be such a phenomenal success! Wait a minute...*You* knew!

Dear Michael,

Yes, I was at the Pepsi commercial filming, that dreadful day in January, 1984. There were a bunch of extras in the front rows and some others hired to wear the Jackson jackets. Nevertheless, I was there. Where else would I have been? It was like we were about to be treated to a free concert. Everything happened so swiftly. We were prepared to be there all day. I think we were only there for an hour after they let us in, if that long.

My friend Irene and I noticed the smoke in your hair almost immediately when it happened. I don't know if she was in shock, but she calmly said, "His hair is on fire...look, Michael's hair is on fire." We looked. We saw. It didn't seem like anyone else had noticed until finally, someone on the stage responded. We could see the smoke, but not the degree of your burn and pain until after you joined God in heaven.

I cried when it happened. I cry even more now about it after seeing this newly released footage. It never appeared that you were as badly burned as you were. And you never let on to me about it. I felt like I could actually feel the fire when I saw that video.

Was this the beginning of the end of your innocence? It doesn't matter now though. You are no longer in any pain whatsoever.

Dear Michael,

It had only been a few months after the Pepsi debacle when Star Magazine called and asked if I was the REAL Billie Jean and if I would interview ... *"WHO TOLD?"*

Not sure who brought them to my attention, maybe one of my friends. I remember someone from Star Magazine called my job. I had never been in front of the media before. It was kind of interesting, but I felt our story was just that...*ours* and who would really care.

While you told me the song was written for me, about me...what was the big deal. I toyed with the idea of the interview and then of course as usual, I came over to the house and you again welcomed me in. Was there really any time that you didn't agree to see me if I came looking for you? Well, other than that incident with your dad that is. Eventually I did stop coming though ....

Anyway, I had come by to ask you if you were okay with my doing the story with Star Magazine.

Your immediate response, "Are they going to pay you?"

I hadn't even thought about that. "I don't know."

"Well do the story only if they pay you. Tell them anything you want and I will back you one hundred percent?"

"Uh Yuh...tell them anything I want huh...what about New York?" I laughed, almost a nervous giggle really.

You smiled, "Let's just keep that personal for now. That will make it harder on you."

"I have every intention to..."

It took a while for me to understand but now I do understand what you meant by making it harder on me. You knew the scrutiny of the press and not just the press, the judgmental people from all around.

When the Star Magazine article came out, I was amazed at the truth that actually was in it, yet I did notice that they took things out of sequence.

Why was I surprised that it was the cover story? Well, the song had been out for a while now and I honestly didn't know what the big deal was. The enormity of Billie Jean was the big deal...silly me!

I called you and you told me to come over to the house and I brought the Star article to you.

"Look at this Michael!" The front page said, "The Real Billie Jean in Michael Jackson's Life and Her Baby" Yeah…you were use to it.

I sure wasn't use to any stories being written about us. We had been in each others lives for over ten years at that point and not too many people knew about the time we shared together.

"You looked at it and said, "Good…by the way, did they pay you?"
"Yes… "
"Great. You should use the money to take care of your son."
Thinking about the kid. I was impressed.

As I look back on it…were you in pain then? You always gave me that one extra mile. I look back and I feel extremely special yet also a little selfish.

You were just going driving that day and asked me if I wanted to go for a ride. You had a little practice with driving at this point so I felt safe enough to do so…LOL…yes I am laughing now, but after that first time riding with you when we were twenty…I was a little leery.

You drove through the back streets of Encino. At this point I knew the area well. You seemed a little sullen, probably wanted to be alone, but let me invade your space again.

Many things were going on in your life. You were having issues with the Kingdom Hall that mainly started when you had to do the disclaimer for Thriller and they were getting on you about hanging out with the kids so much. A sister from the Kingdom Hall told me that I should let my son hang out with you and you will probably pay for him to go to college. So you were being very generous but people were mistaking your kindness.

It was a time when just everyone was still trying to control you and that is why I just thought you were joking when you said, "I am going to become more well known than God."

I don't know how I should have interpreted that. I took it as that would be your attempt.

Yet, perhaps it was just a statement that you believed you would be publicized more than God because that is how good you felt your work was. Who knows?The sad part is it became a reality either way. The distance between us stretched after that. You were beginning to belong to the world now. "Worldly" that is what the Jehovah's Witnesses would call it.

I started letting go. It was time, I thought. I started seeing someone. Yes Michael, the 'star' of my book Obsessions. I guess it was kind of like he replaced you, but in such a different way. No one could ever truly replace you in my heart.

Dear Michael,

By, 1986, I still wrote you but only from time to time and I stopped trying to see you. While, I left you alone, I never totally let go of you. Your career was to the sky. You were becoming inaccessible even to your family.

Some people I knew, that were connected to you musically, kept me in the loop as to what you were doing. Not to mention you were always in the news. By the time I was twenty eight, and a single mom, I was finally ready to move on from the fantasy of you.

...So, do you remember our final ride down Mulholland? Sometime, 1989, if I recall correctly...not so sure...I know you weren't totally living at Neverland as of yet. You had told me the animals were there and that you had to move them because of all the neighbor complaints. Those llamas *were* very smelly!

It was just one of those times we were again destined to just see each other. I saw your brothers at the park every week during softball season. I had been going to the Jackson's and St. Elsewhere's, softball games for several years now.

Many interesting things happened at the Jackson softball games. My friend had a crush on Jackie, but Jackie had his hands full with Enid and Paula Abdul. Randy was in love with Julie at the time and had bought her a four karat diamond ring. Next thing I know he is with a girl name Bernadette. Magic Johnson flew his team out a few times to play against the Jacksons. When he spoke about that at your memorial, the memories came crashing all around me.

My son was getting older and I started dating a man who now possessed my heart. Yes, I know you had the book....couldn't even believe it was me huh ...well, I digress, so let me stay on point here.

My heart was broken at this time and I of course decided I would run back to you.

It wasn't that I was running back to a relationship. I was simply running back to the fantasy of you that always protected me as I was growing up.

Dear Michael...

Do you realize how much we rode in the darn car? (I am laughing here because I truly hated riding while you drove).

I was vulnerable, but you were still there and you were still driving around Encino at night. I had just gotten a brand new car and was driving around too. I was feeling lonely. Where did we meet up at this time? Oh yes, Genesta Park.

Fate, once again, intervened with us. It was really late and when I pulled up to the park - there you sat. I wasn't really looking for you. Or perhaps, subconsciously, I was. We hadn't met at the park in a long, long time. I just wanted to go there and think.

You were just as surprised to see me there. We chatted for a few minutes and then we simply picked up from where we left off as you asked if I wanted to go for a ride. This was our usual, even though it had been a really long time.

"Sure." Really now, what else did I have to do Michael?

You took the back roads once again, but this time up to Mulholland. Yup! You were still driving sporadically, like a crazy person. After this, I vowed to never ride in a car with you again, especially after you took your hands off the damn steering wheel and said, "Sometimes, I wish I was Peter Pan and could fly..." ...uhhh, Michael, you did this on Mulholland Drive...winding roads, major drops...yuh.

"Uh, not with me in the car you don't. Put your hands back on the wheel!" I yelled just as you did. Were you trying to terrorize me Michael?

"I was just playing. You were never in any danger..." you calmed me laughingly.

I had been on a motorcycle before with someone driving like a maniac through those roads. I was fearful of Mulholland Drive.

I don't know what happened to 198VZG (That's what we called your Silver Shadow, maroon and black, Rolls Royce by its license plate), but you were driving a Black Landrover or something like that on this night. At least I can look back at that time and laugh now...I wasn't laughing then mister.

You pulled over into an open, desolate area. Mulholland is known for such spots. At least it use to be. I haven't been there in years.

"I still like to drive up here sometime and just think…" you told me as you laid your seat back and I followed suit. We sat in silence for quite a few minutes. I had closed my eyes, but I could feel you watching me.

I know at this time I had developed a sexiness about me. I was too thin in my own eyes, because I could see the bones in my chest…perfect to the world, but I didn't like it. I had been trying to impress that guy I mentioned early and was working to get him back.

"Where is your son at?" you inquired.

"He's with his dad" I informed you, "he ain't singing that song any more …the kid is his damn son!" I remarked sarcastically.

You laughed. We talked about things that were happening in our lives. Rather, you were more interested in knowing what was going on in mine. I told you about Vincent, my obsession. You told me I shouldn't be with him and not to let him hurt me anymore and to quit doing the crazy stuff I was doing. You did, however, find the story about me and Vincent quite amusing.

Do you remember that I was barely dressed? Cute little baby doll sun dress, braless, fake hair, but it looked real enough. Oh so different than when we first met…You looked handsome, still skinny. You had started to change and it was obvious you had some work done but I liked it at that point. Your skin wasn't changed so much, just a little lighter. I remember at one point we were almost the same shade of brown. Your hair was pushed in a pony tail. I didn't even think about the burn. You had on red pants, white t-shirt.

Should I be talking about this with you in heaven? Well we are all born imperfect and we have sinned many times along the way even though we knew better.

"You have been in my life a long time…" you stated.

"Since we met in Las Vegas in 1974 when we were sixteen." I replied.

"Yeah, but you stopped writing letters. After you first moved here you use to still write and just drive up to the mailbox and put the letters in. I use to see you do that."

"Yeah, well you weren't responding and it was getting harder to see you."

"Well, I didn't respond a lot before and you never gave up. It was just always understood between us. I always allowed you in and that wasn't going to change." Your voice was soft, almost accusatory, as if I truly had abandoned you.

I didn't know how to respond to that, so I didn't. Hell, what, we were thirty years old now. You were more *the* Michael Jackson to me now than you ever were. You were untouchable to most but here we were in a comfort zone with each other as if time had stood still.

Life was moving us on but I still cared about you. I wanted to tell you I kept you in my heart in spite of it all. But I didn't.

I felt the need to reach over to hug you, not sure what you were thinking and as I did, I laid my head on your chest for a few minutes. When I went to move away, you held me tightly and kissed me, completely catching me off guard. After all the time we had spent together, not since that first time had there had been any real intimacy between us other than stolen kisses here and there. Yet, I was quick to respond.

This time our kisses came with an urgency, as if we were trying to recapture innocent moments of what use to be. Both of us seemed to have a strong desire to simply be touched. We weren't so child like this time as our kissing turned into uncontrolled lust. I boldly undid your pants leaving you to remove them as I pulled off my panties. Then I climbed over and straddled you. You didn't seem so innocent anymore either and I had definitely learned to be that bad girl I tried so hard to become. I'd call this a moment of reckless abandonment as we fumbled around inside the truck, caught up once again. Here we were making love like we were in high school. Imagine the media circus had a police car pulled over!

I rested on top of you afterwards. You ran your hand down my hair. We laid there comfortably until my legs began to get stiff and I moved off of you so we could pull ourselves together and straighten out our clothes.

You wanted to stay there for a while longer so we did. I wasn't in any hurry. If you didn't know, I was just happy sitting there with you. I know it was one of a few moments you could just simply be *'Michael'*.

When you dropped me off at my car, we both just smiled. I leaned over and kissed you goodbye. As the gentleman you were, you waited until I got in my car and watched me take off first. There were no promises that I would see you again. We never did that. I knew that we would always find each other along the way, even if to just give a smile.

I never meant to let you down Michael.

Dear Michael,

In 1990, I know you know I gave birth to another son. And I know you are aware that I named him after you, but I liked the way Mychal Thompson of the Los Angeles Lakers spelled his name so I spelled my son's that way.

I was going through such turmoil in my life at the time, and I knew I wouldn't have another chance to give you such an honor because I had decided I wasn't going to be having any more children.

In 1991, I decided it was time for me to leave the San Fernando Valley! I moved to Atlanta. I drove by Hayvenhurst the evening before I left. I felt like I was moving away and on from you.

1993 turned out to be a tumultuous one for both you and me. My mom died. You gave an interview after not having given one in so long and that was to Oprah Winfrey. Ha, she asked if you were a virgin...good answer, "I'm a gentleman". Then in December, you were accused of child molestation. I was torn to pieces, so I know you felt destroyed and that the wind was knocked out of your sail.

I never even remotely thought you were guilty. I knew your heart. God, how I wished you would have fought that battle, but I understood your decision to settle. I know your soul was severely bruised. I sent a letter to you at Hayvenhurst. I figured the fans had Neverland covered. That letter said I believe in you because I know your heart and soul and if you need me, as cliché as it may sound ...I'll be there.

Sadly, you withdrew from the public even more so. Then you married to Lisa Marie Presley. I wasn't feeling it just like everyone else. The kisses didn't seem remotely close to what *we* shared! So I did not buy that public display of affection on the MTV Awards at all.

In 1995, I moved back to California, this time moving to Culver City, just down the street from Sony. Our cars sat at a light together as you were leaving Sony one day. You were in a limousine; I was in my black Honda Accord. You rolled the window down and waved. I blew you a kiss. I wasn't sure if you recognized me or not.

In 1996, you married Debbie Rowe and had some beautiful babies. What were my thoughts? Why her? You and I could have done this a whole lot better and with feelings! That is all I am going to say on that subject.

Dear Michael,

Funny, how even though I moved on to a new obsession, our lives always seemed to intertwine.

When I moved back from Atlanta, I got a job at the accounting firm of Gursey, Schneider & Co. They specialized in entertainment business management and forensic accounting for high profile divorce cases. At first, I was working on high profile divorce cases, to which I was privy to some juicy information. But then they threw me into a production accounting position (of which I had no experience) with Tall Pony Productions.

Name sounds familiar to you huh? Yeah, well that's because you had done several productions with them, but particularly the World Music Awards which they produced. I worked on most of their Sinbad HBO specials.

In mid 1997, I was about to relinquish my position because once again, I wanted out of Los Angeles and was about to move to Phoenix to start my own company. Once I heard we would be working on a Liz Taylor special, I new without a doubt you were going to be there and so would I. It was The Liz Taylor Birthday Celebration, an ABC Special.

The first day you arrived, your security made such a big deal, no one could get to you, but well, after seeing you that first day, Michael, I am sorry, I was truly taken aback. I was upset at your physical appearance. How shallow did that make me?

I felt, "What happened to *my* Michael? I immediately left the venue. I am going to go on the line here and tell you, I barely did any work whenever I was back stage anyway! Especially when I went to Aruba for the Sinbad specials…okay, I am changing the subject again.

I cried all the way home. After I saw you, I remember thinking as well as telling my friends, "If I feel this badly, how must his mother feel?"

Your eyes were so sunken in. Frankly, Michael you reminded me of death, of a corpse. I have always been honest with you, so no need to stop now. Later that night, I realized my shallowness as all my old feelings flooded my heart.

I will see you tomorrow.

Dear Michael,

I was determined I would see you this next day. My badge said "All Access", so dammit, I was going to see you!

But wow, prior to seeing you though, I was sitting in the audience, Nancy, was doing all the work, as I watched the rehearsals.

I just happen to be sitting behind Liz Taylor's people and I nearly threw up in disgust as they sat there saying mocking, horrible things about you. From what I gathered you had brought Prince Michael over to Liz's home earlier. I don't know if it was that day or what but this is what they said,

"Did you see *it*?"

"Yeah that baby is white. Where the hell did he get it from? He is such a freak man. Liz said the same thing. She can't stand him."

"Who the hell would give him a baby anyway?"

I was so dismayed. Such blatant betrayal! I kicked the back of the chair to let them know I was sitting there. At least it shut them up for the moment. I just didn't want to hear it.

Why the hell were you surrounding yourself with these people? I went back stage as soon as they announced over the walkie talkie that you had arrived. Once again security tried to act like I wasn't going to see you…Yeah right…Wayne was running your security.

I knew he was a friend of Jackie's at one point and he was at the Jackson softball games a lot. And he tried to stop me, when he *knew* me! I know, just doing his job right…and that was when you spotted me.

Do you remember…I smiled…you smiled back with once again, instant recognition. "Let her through. Let her through," you told them.

I ran over to you and we embraced in a long tight hug. What wonderful hugs you gave. I hadn't had that feeling in such a long time.

"I missed you…where have you been?" you whispered in my ear, "Where have you been?"

"Always here Michael. Always here."

"How are your sons?" you asked me, again always concerned about the kids.

"Come on Mike, let's go..." they interrupted pulling us apart. No one knew our intimacies, but we did. "Are you going to be here?" you asked me.
"Yes, I'm working on this show. I will be here."

I watched your rehearsal from the side of the stage. You appeared uncomfortable when these little kids asked, "Where is your nose?"
You had on a surgical mask...you told them you had a cold.

My heart ached...I couldn't take it. I went home, knowing you were in there, but looked so different. Do we change so much in seven years?

Dear Michael...

I just wanted to write this time and talk about the VH1 Childhood Secrets of Michael Jackson special....Boy was I mad when they aired that show! Did they not make it seem like I was hunting you down for sex? Like I was some crazed sex starved groupie! How about that?! Like I was some little hussy! LOL, Hmmm was I?

Well okay, we *had* sex in New York...but *they* didn't know and it wasn't like they made it out to be. Damn, we were only nineteen. They called me an old nemesis! When they called and asked me to do the show, I told them only if it was a nice show and not something bad. They promised it would be. I guess that was their idea of nice. Who knows? It was filmed almost a year before you were arrested for child molestation that second time. They waited until the week of the trial to show it.

First off, I should have been aware of the trickery of the industry. I just wrote you about my production accounting experience. I knew a lot of the game. That is why I got out of the entertainment realm. It was too cut throat for me. I just never realized that they would take the actual answers I gave and match them with different narrated questions.

At least I hadn't told them about *our* intimacies. I was happy to keep those simply our memories because once again I know all those special moments, which for you were rare, were times when you could just be *Michael*. I remember before it aired, I was all over those gossip entertainment shows being referred to as Michael Jackson's first girlfriend!

I wondered if you watched it...and when you watched it ...Did you remember the time *we*....

Dear Michael,

By 2003, I very seldom spoke to people about you at this point in my life, but one afternoon I was at my clients, a plastic surgeon, and I was speaking to his wife, well now his ex-wife, who was also his office manager.

We were talking about a term paper I wrote in my Philosophy class that I called, *"The Personal Impact of Michael Jackson on a Life."* I would not have passed that class had I not written that paper.

Anyway, I filled her in on a little of our story, the innocence of it at least. But man, who would have believed that just one week later, you would be calling the doctor's house at 6 a.m. to see if he could see you as a patient.

Of course I received an immediate phone call afterwards. She asked me to come in at the same time so that I could see you. After having read my paper and knowing the actual impact you had on my life, she really just wanted me to see you again.

"I can't do that," I told her, "I was never a groupie for him before and don't intend to be one now. That's just too personal."

"How is it that you are intruding? You work for us. You take care of our money. You can be here."

She honestly just wanted me to see you again. I wanted to be there and I stated that to her, but I just felt like it would have been such an invasion of your privacy. I guess, I felt you had enough of that at the time.

When you went to the surgery center, you signed in under the pseudo name of Michael Jefferson. It wasn't like you were going there for some major surgery, simply some collagen injection...and uhh...you wanted to go under! What the hell Michael, who goes under anesthesia for collagen injection? Is this stuff under HIPA still? With all the other info the media has right now...I don't think so.

But anyway, you know how too, when you tell people you know someone famous they want to see if you are lying...well, hmm that statement doesn't exactly apply to you but you know what I'm saying!

Well, just before they put you under, the doctor's wife went into the surgery room and asked you if you knew who I was. I admit it

Michael. I would have been so hurt if you said no. I guess it was just sort of a validation of all we shared. I don't know.

After you confirmed knowing me, the doctor as a friend, decided to tell you I was diagnosed with a terminal liver disease. According to several doctors, I shouldn't be writing you right now.

You had them give me a message, "Tell her I am praying for her and I'll be in touch." It took you a while, but you did finally call. Hey, what was up with that? Someone, no, not just someone, a doctor told you I was going to die and you took your time about calling me!

Anyway, I guess I can tell you now too, I was told that when you were under, one of the persons working there, no names mentioned, lifted your hospital gown and looked at your *stuff*…that's all I am going to say.

Okay well, after you went to the doctor a couple of times, you hadn't paid your bill. I am laughing about that right now because I was the one who had to do the collection call. Rumors were abounding constantly in the news that you were broke and that you weren't paying your bills!

This was hilarious to me! First, I called Evie who told me she didn't handle that. Evie had been working with you for years at MJJ Productions.

So then I called the cell number you gave them and left you a message.

"Michael" I said in a tone that my nieces say let's them know they are in trouble, "It's Theresa Gonsalves. I need you to pay this doctor bill because they're going to give me a twenty percent collection fee once you pay it and I need to go on vacation!"

Well, even for me it was a surreal shock that your management company called me on my cell phone the very next day and said, "Michael Jackson wants us to make sure the bill you are talking about gets paid immediately. Can you fax it over?"

You know what? It was sent over night delivery! I so loved you for that. And yes, I got the twenty percent! And yes, I used it for vacation! You are too funny. I guess you felt it was business!

I thought back to what you told me when I asked you if I could do the Star Magazine interview… "Are they going to pay you?"

I am sitting here cracking up. Thanks for the memory Michael…blowing you a kiss and my eyes are teary. I will write again tomorrow.

Dear Michael,

Our last face to face meeting, October, 2003...Radio Music Awards, Aladdin Hotel, now called Planet Hollywood...another Tall Pony Production and you were getting an award. Tall Pony invited me because they knew of my feelings for you.

So, as our history has shown, it was inevitable that I would be there...of course I would, where else would I be.

Besides, it was time you met my Mychal. The son I had named in your honor. I am still proud of giving you that honor.

It was a fascinating evening for my son. He was 14 years old at the time. Here he was backstage and waiting to meet you, Michael Jackson, his namesake, someone I had loved all my life, but for him, *"the"* Michael Jackson. You were still, after all these years, favored by even the youngest of fans.

Mychal had been backstage plenty of times in the past. My rule of travel when I did production was that he had to be allowed to come or I couldn't do the show.

He had traveled with me to Aruba, Jamaica, everywhere I went. Mychal had been privileged to meet your sister Janet, Sinbad, Beyonce and he loved it when Natalie Cole told him how cute he was!

At this show, Mychal was running around backstage with his "All Access" badge, meeting Diddy, Murphy Lee, Kelly Rowland, et al, but when I said Mychal, come on it's time for you to meet Michael Jackson, my son got so nervous that he actually chewed up a pen. I mean literally! It was comical.

Just to make me look legit backstage, they gave me some paperwork for you to sign relative to SAG, AFTRA ... or something. My job was to get signatures from you and P-Diddy.

Okay so let me tell you - this was too funny. When I approached Diddy, his people came rushing at me, like he was a superstar or something! LOL...okay, to most he is.

I had Mychal with me and I asked Diddy if he could sign the release documents for the show and he said "NO!"

I looked at him questioningly, like, "Why the hell not?"
He said, "Lot's of people trying to have me served to sue me. I don't sign anything." I laughed at that. Okay, whatever.

So, then I asked him if he would at least give my son an autograph and he said, "Of course."

He takes my son's book, signs it and my being the smart ass that I sometimes can be said, "If I was trying to trick you for a signature, that is how I would have done it!" Diddy laughed. At least he had a sense of humor!

Dear Michael,

It was time for my son to meet you. You, of course, were not aware that I was even there at the moment. I decided to wait until after you received your award. Too hectic before that…this time there was no rehearsal participation for you. It had been a few years again for us and I always wondered if you would still remember me.

Beyonce had given you the award. I was backstage, didn't hear one word you said. Had to look at the shows schedule to even know what the award was for.

When you got off the stage, your entourage and your kids began to follow and then I softly called your name, "Michael."

Amidst all the noise backstage, you heard me. You turned around, "It's me, Theresa…" and it was like time stood still for both of us. It was probably seconds, seemed like hours, but it was like at that moment, no one else was backstage.

You smiled, a smile only you could flash, staring at me in amazement. I knew exactly what you were thinking… "She is still here." Like I said before, *always here Michael. Always here.* I moved toward you, accidentally bumping into one of your kids almost knocking them down and you didn't even notice… then finally my son asked, "Mom, why is he staring at you like that!" Then you finally hugged me and I laughed. Always that comfort between us.

"Hey, I want you to meet my son, Mychal. I named him after you." You smiled and extended your hand to him and you guys shook hands…Damn, where was the camera? Here was my son with you! My life, full circle in front of me and no camera! I flashed a bulb into my memory. Two of your kids were standing with us now.

"How old are you?" you asked him. And he just couldn't answer, he was still so very nervous. You continued staring at me, dead in my eyes for what seemed an eternity and then you me asked, "Are you taking good care of him?"

"Look at him Michael, what do you think?" I responded.

You looked at him.

"I think you are doing a great job."

"Of course I am silly…"

The hustle and bustle began but before they could wisp you away, my son handed you his autograph book and you signed it. You gave me another quick hug and then once again you were gone….My heart, my mind, my soul…flooded with memories that would be the final ones of my seeing you up close and personal…and alive.

"Mom…mom…why was Michael Jackson staring at you like that?" Mychal asked me. I just smiled. And so he went on to tell all of his friends, "Michael Jackson was mesmerized by my mom!"

A couple weeks later you called. You asked about my being sick and I told you about it. Some liver autoimmune thing, they call it Primary Sclerosing Cholangitis. Walter Payton died from it. At this point they don't really know what my problem is. I am an enigma to even the best doctors in the world.

When they had first told me the diagnosis, they said I had three years to live. After finally being released from the hospital after an extensive stay I went home and I took all my Jackson music and played every single song that I have. Every song had relevance to certain moments in my life. When my mom was dying, she said she wanted Good Times to be our family song.

I cried all my fears out at that time. I decided I was just going to live life and decided I was going to have a big party for my 45th birthday because I never had a birthday party. You actually agreed to come. I had to keep it quiet was all you asked. I was already good at that.

You never made it to my party because sadly once again you were arrested for child molestation. I don't really want to discuss it. I believed in your innocence, but was angry at you for making the statements you made during the interview on Sixty Minutes. I knew you were innocent, without a doubt. I just felt you dug yourself into a deeper hole and I sure didn't have faith in our justice system. I so hated Nancy Grace during this time. And even now that you're gone, people of course are still alluding to it. That is not your legacy and we don't need to own it.

You still were persecuted even though found innocent. Makes one wonder about this country that claims you are innocent until proven guilty.

Dear Michael,

I think everyone will remember where they were the day you moved on to eternity.

Me? I was at my doctors' office for yet and still another look at my liver. Yes, a never ending saga for me. I was sitting in the lobby when at 2:45 I received a text from my oldest brother that read, "They just said your boy died." I knew immediately he meant you even though I texted back "Who?" Aloud I said, "Michael Jackson died." My phone started ringing off the hook with both calls and text messages.

Everyone knows I hate the texting thing but they couldn't get me. The nurse took me into an examination room and said, "If it was true, I would have gotten breaking news." I was paralyzed and in shock but somehow I knew it was true. The doctor came in and she told me that CNN was reporting you were in a coma to which I replied, "He's dead. I already know it. He's dead."

I felt it Michael. I didn't want to believe it. I broke down in the heaviest tears I have ever cried in my entire life. The doctor tried to go over my test results with me. I didn't care. I was alive at least and now you were gone. What the hell was going on?

The doctor insisted I stay for a while to calm down. I just wanted to go home. I cried in my car the entire way. I was at least fifteen miles from my house. I had the radio on and all they were playing was you.

I ran into the house when I got home and turned on the news. There stood Jermaine, "My brother, the legendary King of Pop, Michael Jackson, passed away at 2:26 p.m. Thursday, June 25th." I was as lost and empty as most of the world felt.

It was surreal. The pain in my chest - intolerable. Never felt such pain. Again, the tears - unstoppable.

No one wanted me to be alone. My friend Ayshea was first to arrive at my house. As I lay in bed crying, hearing various details on the news, I sat up quickly, unexpectedly and stated, "The doctor killed him." Ayshea turned around surprised by my sudden revelation.
"Why would you say that?" she asked me.
"The doctor let something go wrong. I just know it." I told her and laid back down to an ocean of tears. Ayshea didn't question me. She knew my sixth sense with other things, but particularly with you.

It took five days before the physical pain subsided. And even then, I had to have a drink…an alcoholic one. And with a liver problem, you know, I shouldn't have been drinking. But it helped.

It is hard reliving this day. I am going to go lie down.
I love you forever, Michael….to which I wish I could hear you say one more time

"I love you more!"

August 29, 2009

Dear Michael,

On this day, your birthday, I decided it would be a day of celebrating you and decided it is time to say goodbye to the melancholy and continue instead to smile at all you gave to me and to the world.

You helped my gift of writing make its way to the forefront. A gift I will share forever.

I *was* one of the lucky ones. I enjoyed each and every moment we spent together and I will treasure each and every memory. I thank you for the smiles, the laughs, the songs and the love. You gave me butterflies and good times. My entire life, you were another part of me. You made me who I am today. God, how I want you back! But sadly, it is too late to change the time and so we end up here with your being gone too soon.

I'll be there to defend who you were and dare I say to the world, Michael Jackson, you were a *man*, a great one at that.

I will continue to celebrate your life by doing what you would do…give back.

And Michael, no matter what is said, I will never forget what we did.

Sleep well my prince. I will see you in Glory. Until then, I will see you in my dreams and always remember the time we…

Love Always,

Theresa J. Gonsalves, your real Billie Jean!

Dear Ms. Kate:

I loved your son...not as an icon, but as a man.

Lovingly,
Theresa J. Gonsalves

Dear Reader,

Thanks for sharing this journey with me. I hope this showed you a side of Michael Jackson that you never knew. I truly was one of the lucky ones to have spent so much time with Michael. I wish I had more pictures to share, but when you have access, pictures weren't a necessity. But mostly I wish I would have kept writing him. It seemed to matter.

Since his untimely death, the media speaks mostly of his drug issues. Although Michael was against drugs, he somehow allowed them to grip his being and ended up losing his life. It happens to the best of us and he was the best!

As I deal with this liver disease, mentioned throughout, along with fibromyalgia, I find myself in constant pain. Doctors easily give me pain meds because today it seems doctors bandage the problems instead of really trying to fix them.

I see how easy drugs are available. Don't get me wrong, as I stated in my letters here to Michael, I don't condone the drugs, but I do understand. As, I sit here in September of 2009, I am still suffering from the liver problems. Unfortunately, I have to continue to have surgical procedures and yet I will honestly say the one thing I look forward to is the Propofol ... the going under affect, but always and only, in a hospital environment.

Michael was truly a gift. He gave so much of himself to us. Let's remember his music, his gentle heart, his spirit and his soul. Dance and rejoice about his life…and *remember the time he….*

Theresa J. Gonsalves

Other books by Award winning author Theresa J. Gonsalves

OBSESSIONS – Nonfiction

THE MAN IN THE WOODS – (Fiction)
A three time award winning novel based on a true story.

Coming Soon:

LUCIFER'S MINISTRY

For further information go to: www.theresagonsalves.com

Farewell Michael Jackson
1958-2009